THE UNRETURNING

THE UNRETURNING

MARTIN MALONE

Shoestring Press

Printed by imprintdigital
Upton Pyne, Exeter
www.digital.imprint.co.uk

Typesetting and cover design by narrator
www.narrator.me.uk
info@narrator.me.uk
033 022 300 39

Published by Shoestring Press
19 Devonshire Avenue, Beeston, Nottingham, NG9 1BS
(0115) 925 1827
www.shoestringpress.co.uk

First published 2019
© Copyright: Martin Malone

The moral right of the author has been asserted.

ISBN 978-1-912524-20-4

ACKNOWLEDGEMENTS

Acknowledgements are due to the following publications, anthologies and online journals in which some of these poems, or versions of them, first appeared: *Acumen, Agenda, And Other Poems, Angle, The Attic Sessions #14, Bare Fiction, Blackbox Manifold, Book 2.0, Causeway/Cabhsair, Coast to Coast to Coast, Dream Catcher, Eborakon, Elbow Room, The Fat Damsel, The Frogmore Papers, The Galway Review, Gutter, Haverthorn, Iota, Long Poem Magazine, Lighthouse, The Moth, Nutshells & Nuggets, Orbis, Poetry Film Live, Poetry Ireland Review, Poetry Pacific (Canada), Poetry Salzburg Review, Poetry Spotlight, PORT, Prole, The Reader, Route 57, Stand, Under The Hedge, Under The Radar*. Also, *To cross the wine-dark wave: Poems for the Hartlepool Bombardment Centenary, The Ecchoing Green: poems inspired by William Blake, Orkney Writers' Course Anthology 2017, Truths: A Telltale Press Anthology 2018* and the *Hands & Wings* anthology. 'Mrs. Mounter' won the 2012 Mirehouse Poetry Competition. A number of these poems appeared in my pamphlet, *Mr. Willett's Summertime* (Poetry Salzburg, 2018) and six of them first appeared in my collection *Cur* (Shoestring, 2015), they are included here because of a thematic link to the book's main subject, which is not Pity.

Thanks to: Pam Beasant, Vega Brennan, Matthew Campbell, Niall Campbell, Helen Dewbery, the late Helen Dunmore, Jonathan Edwards, Dawn Gorman, Wolfgang Göertschacher, Mick Gowar, Jen Hadfield, Keith Hutson, Richard Jobson, Charles Lauder Jnr., John Lucas, Helen Lynch, Fíonn Malone, Erich & Angelika Markwica, Dan O'Brien, Elizabeth Pender, Mariette Evina-Purcell, Adam Piette, Michael Symmons Roberts, Peter Robinson and Jen Shaw. Thanks are due, also, to Aberdeen City Council, who gave me funding towards a number of residencies during the course of writing and editing this book, and to the National Trust for Scotland who commissioned the poem 'War And The Farmer'.

CONTENTS

II   THE UNRETURNING

I

Ghosts of the Vortex

"Those images that yet
  Fresh images beget"
                    – W.B. Yeats, 'Byzantium'.

SEANCE

Date yourself 2014 and come;
by now it is only language
and low opportunity
calling witness
to provide
the necessary
authenticating element:
a scrawled utter
of utterness,
trench honesties
occluded by one century
and the paradigms of myth.

Even then, you had to lie.
With the advantage
of immediacy,
small wonder
the shires were sad,
small wonder
the corpse-constructed line
found its pitiful page.
What they said of it
became what it is,
though the terms to describe
do not exist.

So come,
let us sit and reconstruct;
the glass on the table
historian enough
to catch their words
and stop this rain,
to stop this rain,
to stop this rain.

MIDSUMMER

As though nothing happens
our hemisphere shoulders the sun,

the hill asleep on its trove of peat,
the sea is soaked in light.

In the days before Johnsmas
we bear fuel to the *sgùrr*,

our own brief blaze stoked
in its hours and seasons

by the darkness and the light.

MRS. MOUNTER CIRCA. 1914

You have seen them come and go: the salesmen,
stevedores, undergraduates and tinkers,
lorn veterans of Omdurman and Colenso,
the struggling artist with his curious hours;
all passing through the widow's breach of spare
room. Your years lived impasto—caked-on,
palpable as Sunday Best—are rendered boldly,
dealing only in certainty, creed and nation,
dealing solidly in bricks and mortar
and the definite vertical of the doorway
that frames you as you sit, impassive
as the teapot, immovable as the rent.
Outside the world turns to mud, feeds its sons
to fire and lead and the names
you will hear for the first time:
Passchendaele, Somme, Ypres, Mons....

LET US SLEEP NOW

Vienna, 31/7/2014

Then you spot him after all these years,
on the U3 platform at the *Westbahnhof*
heading out towards Simmering.

You glimpse his profile in the tunnel's gloom
but can't quite root that lean face,
clean and good-looking and well again.

The heatwave's been good to him,
tanning his skin caramel and free
of the pallor of your last strange meeting.

A tattooed bicep strains impressively
at the t-shirt, a booted calf flexes
and there he stands in his animal prime.

You smile with recognition, catch his eye;
not Saxon or Prussian or Pomeranian
just an Austrian boy heading west again,
not your way but up the line to Simmering.

SORLEY'S BULLET

"Books and bullets have their destinies"
— Ernst Jünger, *Storm of Steel*

And so it finds you, like many another,
late for your own last rites, a lean lad
running the downs to Hackpen Hill,
hair lank with rain, mind made up
and homing in on College supper.
We can't say you'd not told us,
nor pretend you didn't leave behind
advice for times like these: say only
'They are dead' and so it is.

And so it finds you, like many a better,
biting the bullet and doing your bit,
with just enough paper to thank a teacher
and Arthur for his tale of meeting Wells.
Return that New Testament to store, take only
your Homer and the Kennet's pagan drift
through the veins of a final Summer,
as you walk your weathers from Avebury
to Adam's Grave. For so it is.

Lending yourself to the cross hairs
you lean out to fix a sandbag, ghostless
and young, given only to the task at hand
just south of the Hohenzollern Redoubt.
Gently, you slide forward as in easeful sleep,
and it is all as one: detached as Socrates,
sacrificed as Christ, guilty as Barabbas;
none come back, at least not for long.
Say only, 'They have gone'. And so it is.

SHOTS

Odd
how the angle of shot
eases you towards
an allegiance.

As if
your eye seeks
                        beyond the frame
for the horizon
            and sees in it
their unattainable tomorrows.

Black & white
            only increases affinity
for the rear view of crouching men
edging forward into partial middle distance;
some running, one falling forward,
always away from you.

Before me
their various exits:
stage left, Tommy Atkins
to his Great War,
                        stage right
            Frontschwein
to Der Erste Krieg
            while upstage
Le poilou drops face down
into myth-embracing
Verdun mud.

And none of them can look you in the eye.

MACHINE-GUN HONEYMOON

For the new Mrs. Nevinson

One week in The Shambles and his Futurism's
a thing of the past, so with time running
out we decide to put it in writing.

It rains hard, he's cut his hand, I'm late
and in Room 13 stands the registrar
with our glum-faced families.

My new father-in-law's out in Gallipoli
but leaves us his car, with its
ludicrous gas bag on the roof.

Then dinner and third-class to Ramsgate
for the queerest of honeymoons.
I put up with it, one does:

"the most beautiful woman in London"
and her Vorticist private,
the painter of smells.

He's seen things we may have to get used to,
deals in paint with a need to forget
the clarity of a central idea,

the shrieks, pus, gangrene and the disemboweled.
So everything is locked into place,
the living figures hemmed

in by their stockade of wooden beams, the jagged sky
barred by an interlocking web of wire
and man becomes machine.

Man becomes machine and I have my rival in love,
the most beautiful woman in France,
as men fall for *La Mitrailleuse*.

PHOEBUS APOLLO

i.m. Julian Grenfell

Warm with late spring, in a field near Ypres,
you were never happier than on this big picnic,
chatting with the General when that shell struck.

For you it was a job you'd a flair for and loved,
and, when the Great War finally came,
permission to hunt the biggest game.

If your Dad twice swims Niagara and shoots
everything that moves, what else is a well-bred boy
to do but stick pigs in India and dream of Troy?

Long, long before a love of Homer and boxing gloves,
habitual peril was the deal cut for privilege:
yours, then, but the tribal code witnessed in blood.

As with all sport, you took to it well, bagged a laurel;
found increase in battle, love in the taking of life,
and gilded your game book with three Pomeranians.

O Sarpedon! O Hotspur! Your burning moment broke
upon the grubby *kudos* of shrapnel, its splinter driven
an inch-and-a-half into classically educated brain.

And 13 days later, the languid death in a curtained room
stricken with sunbeams, holding Mummy's hand, serene
enough to trim a *Krupp*-made end with Phoebus' gold.

TRENCH REQUISITES

In my old soldier manner, I told him he'd soon
change his style, but he'd shrug and not listen.
So, we share out the hamper left behind,

while another makes good his transition
from man to riven thing. On our minds,
the memory of a Christmas that waxed forever

over eighteen months of deadlock and shellfire,
as King & Country turns to *Quand sera-ce fini?*
and Intha Pink, once in-the-line, is growing old.

Yes, how we hate you, you cheerful young men
with your tinned kippers and today's *Daily Mail*;
the periscope from Harrods, the warm new boots;

galoshes bought yesterday in Knightsbridge;
your wire-cutters and quail eggs from Aunt Grace,
and Father's gift of an Aquascutum.

You'll get used to the smell of blood and rum,
soon learn to see, beyond the metaphors of dawn,
the blue smoke from his bacon frying and know,

here at the suicide of nations, not to chance a look.
Learn fast and perhaps you might live to out-ghost
the silence of your name hallooed twice at roll call.

KNIGHT ERRANT, 1915

A spitted dragoon
prone in pike-grey,
Oskar Kokoschka considers his fate
and wonders if you can paint premonitions
or, in the war of endless coincidence,
is this just another incident
bereft of the brush
to anoint a meaning?

As March canvass turns
August into wounds,
his lung swabs blood
from the jag of Russian bayonet
and things begin to swim,
heading out towards allegory
and revenant self-portrait:
Eloi, Eloi, lama sabachthani?

He floats above himself as seraphim,
notes a passing influence of Grünewald
and the Northern Renaissance,
while Mahler's widow looks on,
sphinx-like, close attendant
to his ever-present grief
and the narrow horizontal
of a stricken son of man.

AN-SKY'S LAMENT

When the coffeehouse war turns real,
we are where we have always been,
which is everywhere
and nowhere,

armed to the teeth with jokes,
adrift on our salty sea,
fed by the blood-rushed rivers
of a vagrant history.

I write down every story,
record every tragic tale,
note each sardonic nugget
slung into the face of shame,

that we may have a memory
—in the days of our affliction—
narrate our own catastrophes
in *Poilen* and in *Galitsye*.

Awake, Lord! Why do you sleep
while our enemies, at their leisure,
set brother to fight brother?

You have made us a byword among the nations,
a laughing-stock among the peoples.

A Jew in every army
between two worlds.

THE TURNIP WINTER

When nostalgia is a healthy tayter,
you know you're in for a hard winter.

So, the war bread squats mud-frog before us,
the clay of stars grown cold on prayer

refusing its miracle of change. Soon
we open up our own front on farmsteads

and orchards, each victory celebrated
in apples, *brötchen* or the medal of an egg,

the shrapnel of lost husbands briefly gone
in a ruckus of fed children. Field-grey ghosts

say grace at our table and turnip, turnip, turnip,
heavy as bad news, becomes this weevil grief

that gnaws through the fabric of our days.
Swede soup for breakfast, swede chops for lunch,

swede cake for dinner. Dried turnips ground
for drink so *ersatz* we lose what it's meant to be.

One day I shall steal home enough bacon
in my bloomers to be again their mother.

One day, the blockade will lift and gobbets
of you will counterfeit their father.

MASSENGRÄBER

Mass graves sink into the solitude of lowland heath.
Dark pines stand beyond the heather and sand.
Wan-blue sky hangs high above barren hamlets.

Low white clouds scud by, shadows sunk
to greet the dead below, comrades drifting
face-down or beached upon the final strand.

Mass graves scatter this land
as strange birds circle above, black-feathered, mournful,
searching the hours for lovers lost that longed-for home.

They sing the elegy of mothers, of brides that-never-were,
laments of man and child for dead ideas of duty.
Their bootless feet but scarcely tread the earth:
frail clay, lame and unformed for rest.

Eyes black, with the pearl's tearful lustre,
their torn hearts shimmer from gaping chests.

So they fly, circling land and sea. And the seldom cry
of disconsolate joy rings out, as a bird finds its love's goal,
knowing that the love lies buried where the blood flows.

Once more it sings to an end the lay of unknown men,
and ever more crimson runs the heart's wash into dry cracked earth.
The dying bird lies on the grave, a black cross of raised head
    and spread wings.

The song becomes softer now—a psalm of return, wounds and
    resurrection—
until it dies away and, at home, a final mother dries her tears.

THE 1ST WOMEN'S BATTALION OF DEATH

At Bochkareva's petition, Karensky signs off
on the Women's Battalion of Death.
Loath and weary of war but quick enough
to grab a peasant's tit, it's a last-ditch bid
to shame broken men back into battle.
Sent up the line near Smorgon, ordered over
the top, lads dither while the girls leave them
behind, pushing on to the German trench
where women well used to drunken fists,
break the trove of vodka before their men
can uncork. This is not fit work for farm girls
and maids who block the path to our retreat.

Like tossing hay onto a cart, that big lass
with her bayonet tears the guts from a Saxon,
and suddenly formations muster everywhere:
1st Petrograd, 2nd Moscow, the Kuban Women's
Shock Brigade yet others without sanction,
charging into action like a new world order
where we don't matter. Of course, you know
what will happen when the lads take a drink.
Karensky won't save them nor will renown,
their medals and good conduct mean little
to drunks and the Tsar will soon be gone.
So, if the boys want fight, you better let them.

WANTON BOYS

Seventeen is not a grateful age
but they'll take you young, over-
look your lies for a roaring engine

so, you swap these carefree years
for the freer sky's new testament
of *nacelle, Pitôt, ailerons, magneto...*

A dream, conjecturable as heaven,
flight's still fresh miracle paints
its brilliance across your days,

and earth grows suddenly remote
while cirrus turns copper, fades pink
then drifts away grey into night.

Thiepval, down past Boiselle, round
the Fricourt salient and on to Mountauban,
the earth taking moonlight like moleskin,

then home to dinner and the empty chair
of a boy you'd laughed with over lunch,
lost at two thousand feet where he worked

the arc of our own guns. Summer weather
brings days of blue and crystal, heat bumps
throwing us up above the haze to circle

like flies in an August room, the air
our element over the guns' continual
scintillation. From here the land

is shorn of its contours and the PBI
but dun figures labouring under kit
while we move like spirits in an airy loom.

Always in your blind spot, it is chance
we fear most: aberration, tailspin,
fire or the unforeseen.

You die alone in the clouds
and death, like the sun, is a thing
you cannot gaze on too long.

MR. WILLETT'S SUMMERTIME

An Act to provide for the Time in Great Britain and Ireland being in advance of Greenwich and Dublin mean time respectively in the summer months. Date of Royal Assent: 17th May 1916.

Where to begin with time? Rise early, saddle a horse and ride
out to Petts Wood. The morning, incandescent with summer,

is running over itself to get at it and it and it and daylight
is everywhere wasted on sleepers beyond drawn down blinds.

It's for toil and lovers you would save this, though the times
beat you to it, grab the minutes for coal and zero-hours

that fuel a different summer. Now we've time to die
over and over before our letters reach home

and afterwards doesn't always come behind before,
if at all. So, the barman calls 'Time!', the whistle sounds

and, after synchronising our watches, we move off
around the point you notice that loosening cough.

1916, and, like many a medal, your moment arrives
post-mortem, the blinds still drawn in Petts Wood.

NEVERENDIANS

From half-term Indians to hard-nosed veterans
in the space of a year, underage and over here,

we hunker down beneath a ridge lousy with Fritz
and know in our bones it's the war that wins wars,

that blood alone moves the wheels of history and that
this trench system, set end-to-end, might circle what

we like to call God's Earth, His good work spoiled
by the hand of man which, having written, moves on

in a scrawl of broken men but again finds time,
when out of the line at the end of a bloody day,

to slump into a dug-out, once more take up its pen
and wearily address the hopeless task of this:

It is my sorrowful duty to write to you of the death
of your son...

UNTITLED

After Pierre Jean Jouve

The man who'll be dead tomorrow
may die no more today.
He'll listen to his heart beating
in the immensity of his flesh;
and the million blue suns
that can gild a single night,
are not beyond his hopes.

Unable to recall what it's like
to have never killed a man,
could he, himself, be dead,
breathing deep the darkness?

BIDDEN

After Mary Bordern

Here are cotton things
and rubber things;
here, liquids and pots.
Here are steel things
and pillows; tin boxes,
needles and glass.
Here, are labels and little
white squares of gauze.

Yes, I know
that you understand these things
but it doesn't do to think.

You pile blankets
onto his wasted body;
fetch jugs of hot water;
boil long rubber tubes
in wretched saucepans.

Their courtesy as they die,
reluctant to cause me trouble
or put me out, as I gauge
how fast a life is ebbing.

Some hurry,
chasing a last omnibus,
for others, there is no such rush,
as if savouring the slow throes
of their own obliteration.

His brain comes off in my hands
as I lift away the bandage,
Death annoyed at my fussing.

I know you understand,
but what have you
and all these things
to do with the dying
of this man?

Nothing.
Take them away.
Release has entered the room
and a miracle draws near.

MALLORY

Yours a fate of inescapable context:
that last climb and its slow ascent of lore
to our shared guess at the outcome.
Strachey's 'unimaginable English Boy',
wasted as a teacher, whose friendliness
offends those Charterhouse lads bound
for Passchendaele. Here ahead of them,
you stand beside your howitzer, look out
across Picardy and long for mountains
where time is other, and eight years
pass like low cloud skimming you to
apotheosis. You glance at your watch
awaiting the hour. Back in England now
young Irvine's still abed at Shrewsbury,
dreaming of the Second Step, Ruth is
home with Frances Clare and all's fair
in Godalming. In the face of a westerly,
the pilot zone calls back today's target.
A tug on the rope, the screaming glissade
and wire-cutting begins on the Somme.

RETHEL

After Wilhelm Klemm

Solemnly the night's smoke rises
from the rubble of gutted factories.
Rose moonlight swaggers, lovely-mad,
over broken brick mountains as

the column is swallowed by dismal streets.
The moon plays up high on a ruined façade,
flitting night-blue through vacant windows,
ducks itself behind reckless gable-ends.

Now the ravaged town gleams deathly white:
a white of horror, the pallor of silence.
And the grey-ghost helmets of a dark army
roll through midnight, muffled wave upon wave.

WAR AND THE FARMER

i.m. Major James Keith of Pitmedden, Aberdeenshire

When it comes to war,
your farmer's a useful sort
and I have had no other hobby.
Each acre has to pull its weight,
the supply of heroes maintained,
and heroes, in turn, must be fed,
ergo three-seventh in oats,
one-seventh in roots
and grass for the other three;
meat, milk, potatoes and bread
cake with bran for the dairy,
and cattle, not sheep, mainly cattle.
          In my life,
I am little heroic
but do, always, what's needed
before I'm compelled, so
when each man has to pull his weight,
I go out with the earliest outgo—
howitzer, limber and six-horse team,
Festubert, Passchendaele, the ridge at Messines,
clear guidance at home for my grieve:
three-seventh in oats,
one-seventh in roots
and grass for the other three;
meat, milk, potatoes and bread
plentiful bran for the dairy;
close, darkening lanes,
our hushed-up wrongs
and cattle, not sheep,
always cattle.

RIPON WORK

They are dying again at Beaumont Hamel
as you stroll Borage Lane,
three days after your twenty-fifth birthday,
mind yet cobbled with skulls of the lads you left behind.

Spring is pushing back through the hedgerow
with lesser celandines

and along the banks of the Skell,
a kingfisher's lyddite triggers
that ghost of a twitch.

At number seven, you unlatch the gate,
take out a key and stroll up to the white front door.

Searching for peace, you retreat to the attic with its tiny skylight,
the shrieks of children playing soldiers down on the street.

Here you are Chatterton and Keats,
half in love with death's idea
while making best use of its dutiful shadow.

You write your mother, go over old drafts,
'defectuousities', and 'the inwardness of war'.

Briefly, you pause to listen to swallows *skirruping* their early return,

then back to your notes, strike-throughs,
séance and retrospection,
another time-strafed Edwardian
caught out in the open with defective kit.

The town's darkening lanes are kind to you,
gift you a send-off
and, here, sensing how it all will end,
you teach yourself to carry your cross.

THE BISON'S IDEA OF PLEASURE

i.m. Saki

In the *estaminet* of the Fortunate Rabbit,
you find yourself lending matches
to a man working hard on the square egg.
He claims to be a victim of the war,
before going on to recount a tale
of the visionary brought low by sharp practice
and a cunning aunt. *Some of you English
are men of private means, are you not?*
Then the request for a loan of eighty francs;
an opportunity for which you give thanks
but decline in favour of marriage to his aunt.
Biting muddy biscuits with muddy teeth
among chance-foregathered men,
you later consider, for the mud of a moment,
a badger's-eye view of the honeycombed earth,
dwelling, at length, upon all that is not *estaminet*.
And all that is not *estaminet* is mud
and the bison's idea of pleasure:
muck-bath, hell-broth, quagmire, filth,
engulfing you as cheese engulfs cheesemite,
knee-deep and greasy to souse you for hours, days, weeks.
The streaming clay walls of a narrow-dug support trench
when thaw and heavy rain have come atop a frost,
send you to your hands and knees in the dark,
crawling through the thick soup of mud to a dug-out
where you stand deep in mud, lean against mud,
grasp a mud-slimed fork with mud-caked fingers,
clearing clay from your ears, winking mud from your eyes
which close upon a grit-free instant's dream of warm beds,
fresh eggs and the guileless quiver of a maiden aunt.

JANUARY 10TH, WORLD WITHOUT END

After Helen Thomas

Christmas has come and gone
and today has paid me out,
paling into stoppage time
when the heart beats only.
The snows lie deep
under trees that moan
as if woeful at his going.
The clock has stopped
and I mark time in things
to store against my lack:
the eyes, sad smile and touch,
the tremor in his voice
that is my undoing.
We move about the house
as ghosts, dread-separate,
torn between our agony
and fear of it showing.
I weary for some warmth,
some sound, some colour
against the endless grey
but spring does not lift
into blue-again skies.
He mans himself in fatherhood,
takes the children out
to help him saw the big tree
blown down at our door.
At evening he undresses me
and reads to me until
the fire burns down,
hand on my breast, voice low.
He cannot see my face.

TANK

After Pierre Jean Jouve

martian machine
—double-jawed tower—
with your fiery skull
where lives man's calculus

from each side burst shrapnel
shells, life-devouring bullets
as you stomp over earth
upon living, dying and dead

compress the trench beneath your jounce
as you'd close two sides of a wound

blind beast
rampant in the battle's blast
                  beyond even the vanguard

—inside,
the heroes
padded up to the nines,
hurl at walls to smash their courses
firing and killing on all sides,
burnt by the torrid heat of engines
deafened by the din of exploding iron
living their last day

here's the child of their divine brain
here the bright clarity of our world

HANGERS

You pick your way through his last things,
aware that you are struggling.

And here's this, just wood and metal pins.
What else off which to drape a ghost?

Rubberstamped 23116988: one brother,
conscript, Private, standard-issue.

Failing to clear some sense of anniversary,
you put it back on the rail and close the door,

then polish a cap-badge, put his medal
in your pocket and head for the beach;

thoughts of your last conversation worn
against the silence. How it ended, hanging...

WOOD ON THE DOWNS

After Paul Nash

We have been here before. Uffington, Hackpen,
Grim's Ditch, Ogbourne St.George, Wayland's Smithy,
Sparshott Firs, Bishopstone and Barbury;
all the trodden way from Overton
to Beacon Hill. Each place its *genius loci*,
a favourite colour: Ash-Blue, Ochre,
Payne's Grey, Terra-Verte, Lamp Black, Sienna.
But today you ditch your winter tones
and bid for late spring. The trees are in leaf,
the chalk from the downland reflects light
from a milder sky. *Through field glasses*
one sees a landscape that one can see
in no other way. Here, then, is yours:
the stiff cilia of trunks—a brown-fringed
platoon lost on Hill 60—ghosts of the vortex,
the leaching colours of pending summer,
the breast, lumbar and hip curve of hill
prone upon the bed of Buckinghamshire.
And there I join you eighty years away,
with my Trojan girl; lifting her face
to mine in the dappled light of the wood.
We have been here before.

NOSTOS

To each hamlet a homecoming
and the ghost story it brings.
This, a slow train hauling back
the nightmare of Verdun
on his still muddy boots.
Unexpected as May frost,
step heavy under the weight
of all he's seen since leaving
the farm to a young wife,
he stops off for cognac
in a neighbourhood bar,
where few recognize
the war-altered face.
Ariége boy, home on leave,
do you pause on the track
to *Le Quié*, breath again
that ripe air of the hill's acres,
gorge on estranged silence
then stiffen to the breeze
which leads you back to her?
I see you now in the wood
above *Jacquet*, in a moment
closer than thought to one
raised in the shade of its pines.
You turn for home, hitching
your weariness onto shoulders
robbed of love, these final steps
to take you out of hell.
Poilu, they will kill you,
for what you do
to what you find
upon that bed.
They will track you down
and shoot you
for running.

PENSIVE HEAD

After Wyndham Lewis

What is it about that Thirties palette?
Those browns, a decade-long autumn endlessly
taking leave of the branch: stoic farewells
on steam-swamped platforms, pensive heads
opaque through café windows; ducking down
to order soup through hatches, fingers like
rheumatic sausages prop sallow faces
bent over the tea cup of thwarted lives.
As if the brush knew what was coming,
as if it hunkers down in the spectrum's
trench: a reflex wrapped in khaki, nurtured
in mud and want. Of eyes that have witnessed
too much; that have seen the peacock's head
held under Brown Windsor, shot off above
the parapet of, say, ochre. At the quayside,
dirty hankies wave goodbye to the red
neckerchiefs bound for Aragon, stand back
to let the tanks pass, wave through the ranks
of goose-stepping shirts; yes, those shirts.

ARCHIVES

After Christian Boltanski

We are all so complicated,
                 then die;
 from one stage pass quickly
to the next, become
        objects that were someone.

The eye seeks out pattern and is satisfied.
What can you see
        in a darkened room:
ten columns of three,
saints' bones for the century?

Each one has his own life,
            each her own story:
the children of Dijon,
      unknown person,
stolen graduates of Vienna.

Into every eye shines a light,
      its wires trailing clumsily
down the wall,
and beneath each face,
      a tin box for the soul.

DEAR REVISIONIST

Thank you for your neo-concern
that we grasp the full facts
of this complicated matter;
for sending out, once again,
the officer class to explain
the subtle difference between
Blackadder and the nation's history,
the one being truth the other comedy;
for pointing out our parents' mistake
in taking *Oh What A Lovely War!*
to be anything but a sixties musical
and not how it really was. Thank you
for assuming our poetry stops at Owen;
for sending out the privately educated
to explain that confusion in the ranks
between your national story
and literature's false history,
as if, not royal families, but poetry
tips men into war graves.
Saxe-Coburg, be advised, your poppy
                    is not mine.

I'm grateful to you for letting me hear
Paxman attempt the phrase *wor canny bairns*.
And I do appreciate your engagement
with those events which legitimise
the contemporary state of affairs,
or, as you put it on a recent visit
to a sink school, *make pride cool again*.
I appreciate, as you say, the need
to understand the popular thinking
of the day; how words you are trying
to re-claim meant something real
to my grandfather right up to that morning

the Liverpool Regiment came unstuck
at Hermies, on the road to Cambrai.
As if history can make some
long term sense of the losses
and every lesson to be learned
is, once more, yours.

II

The Unreturning

"It would be interesting to know how we shall
  ennoble our new media as we have already
  ennobled and made significant our old—candle-
  light, fire-light, Cups, Wands and Swords, to choose
  at random."

— David Jones, Preface to *In Parenthesis*.

'14

1 *The Versus Habit*

You feel the need to go back and honour them, take on board their *sacred duty*; lap up *Glory* like news from home and sit down with their sacrifice, as real to them as the waste seems to us. At their most modern, they took the selfies of their day, addicted with good reason, to the ever-present now: poses held in the camera's funk, diaries of the deep-drowned ditch. Later come the memoirs and their small fictions of memory, the versus habit hard to kick. Today you can get all this in the palm of your hand. The foreground is different but the background's up for grabs. They are our ghosts.

Prized assets of a ghost economy, we stand-to awaiting the orders of the day. Your quartermaster kits us out in party shades of khaki, issues plans for our deployment, draws down budget lines, hitherto unseen, across the broad front of commemoration. There's going to be a show and everybody knows it's the big one. Shapeshifters all, we photo-bomb your every opportunity to rebuild bridges back to what is missing; to that unironic register of old words sweet upon your tongue. For, a nation dies when its gods are dead. The new one, then, is this, your profit our loss.

So, when you took this sweet ride for its June spin were you stoked on the cut of your own dumb dash? Did you fail to consider how the casual and throwaway can come out of nowhere, take a wrong turn into the motorcade and catch you by the toe with its brace of lucky shots? A hole blown into that buff bodywork, the itsy tear just an inch below your brocade collar, as the Tschakos and Tschapkas react too late, and the doctors lose ten minutes cutting open a jacket while those words stick in your throat. The Gräf & Stift Double Phaeton: now *that* is what any bloke would call top gear and everyone remembers where they were when you bought it.

It's the last thing I learn before nothing wraps me in metaphor written-white. He stands, smiling at the joke, on the threshold of wherever-it-is-we-go: 'My friend, irony too has ghosts.' The accent's pronounced though his English sound: 'Please, follow me.' So, I track him down some dull tunnel to a warehouse full of firsts: lovers, kisses, early losses. Pushing on through a queue of the recently-gone, I recognize a knot of fellow passengers. One nods back. Brought down by stray ground-to-air, who knows what snug maxims will wind up on the wire of your own demise? 'You think you had it bad.' He wrings out his shirt, lights a fag then tells me of the *Amphion*.

5 *Hartlepools*

A hometown drifts in on the haar, endures in memorable information as answer to the security question for a damp December morning. On the Headland, this day's unknown stretches back beyond the fog bank, further out than Dogger and German Bight, to the bridge moored off Heligoland where an Admiral scrolls up his chart. Hipper's gamble needs no re-tweet, it's been coming for weeks and everyone knows that needs to know and they know better than to tell them that don't. At ten-past eight and 17-years old, Hilda Horsley is a tailor on her way to work when the shell paints her Guernica. By half-past she is soul-sack and older than time.

And so it lives on long after your genes have dissolved into the deep beyond Marwick Head: Edwardian adversative, Junker's bane, stern patriarch of the call-to-arms. Shouldering past Omdurman, burying blame for that dearth of shells, your immortal soul is now a Field Marshal's cap, thousand-yard stare and the waxed moustache. Leete's icon points the way to manhood, Thiepval and a field-won name. Answering the want, see how they came, a volunteer army raised on hoardings, omnibus, tramcars and shame: off whistling for their shilling along the track of your gaze. It is still considered masterful. They have still not returned.

Not that iconic shot of him wrapped in his blanket, outstretched hand feeding petals to the lens, but a black & white taken by the sea, arms hidden inside a trench coat. Younger, he is yet carrying shades of the Mem Hall with its *Sed miles*, still willing to play up and play the game. A face seen so many times on the broad High Street; flushed with plenty, old before its time, dying the thousand deaths of duty. It is noted in tones of some surprise that, towards the end, he thought to join the infantry. But by then the star-shell of his five minutes had caught him out in the open, frozen in the forward sap of the Festival Hall, Rodney and Molly already reaching for the blinds at *Far Leys*.

8 *Flash Mob*

Assembled of a sudden, we watch them go in the name of a hobby or the honour of their school, to the credit of their trade, for the roots of a name, for the streets of their town, for the *kudos* of the game: Tyneside Irish, London Welsh, Arts & Crafts, West Belfast, Stockbrokers, City, Public Schools, Bicycles, Football, Battersea, Hull, Bankers, Bristol, Bradford, Leeds, Sheffield, Rhondda, Salford Pioneers, shoulder-to-shoulder the Empire League, it's yeoman-and-yeoman and King's Own Bowmen for Brave Little Belgium and on into Berlin; the ten-street armies mustered by their masters are here because they're here, because they're here because…

And because of this you hold fast to your Achilles, your Crécy and Gawain, your Agincourt and Blenheim. With an all-the-same blush but the due of a chap drawn close to his own inescapable fact, you ride out the dog days of that fabled summer as if to hunt. One only lives once, so play up and live it well and, if you must, die better, an English knight impeccably dispatched upon the plain of Ilium, blood-elegant in the still sad music of your final dismount, as your horse is torn throat to gut by six rounds from a *Spandau 08*. Get to your feet, slip in warm viscera and, on the way down, take one of your own through that finely sculpted jaw. ROFL. ROFL? Not anymore.

10 *Truces*

So many since the war to end all need of them, but nice that our own abides to offload groceries one hundred years on. The handshake, the chocolate bars, swapped baccy and badges—those jumpers for goalposts—all snug in the myth kitty divvied up for Christmas by this flawlessly whiskered troupe. Here, no rats feast on body parts, depiction is fictional, though achingly done, and everything's based on historical fact. How shall we now witness those others from wars that didn't happen: the unremarked ceasefires of Dhofar, Derry, Sierra Leone; the gables, rough diamonds and dead *adoo* propped up as warnings in the souk at Salalah?

15

11 *Fake News*

Alternative facts from the mouths of the righteous. 80,000
Russians across from Archangel, snow on their boots and roubles
to burn in the station bars south of Leith; a company of zombie
deserters alive between the lines; the Agincourt bowmen re-
strung for St. George; the Crucified Canadian; those angels at
Mons and Tommy as Christ, all looking on while Fritz renders
the dead into tallow: roadside calvaries to that which is true.
Meantime, the monstered mask profiteer's guilt as up on the
moon sits a bomber from the war we've yet to fight. And, in this
banqueting hall of the dis-informed, the Führer rocks his
sling-backs while comedians feast on hamster.

12 *The majority illusion*

Don't wander off to chew berries with the enemy and stay within your primate group. When the world is not enough, just pack up your troubles and do your bit for the augmented reality of this, the narrow trench of a new taxonomy. It is, after all, what everyone thinks, the need self-evident in the hashtag bunker of Northcliffe's *Times*. The long uneven lines roam impatiently towards their fancied majority, wordless, distracted and lost or about to be. Bayonet pokermen go to your glory remembering that the best lines hold. Just walk towards the foe, who is no longer there you have our word. The basic training ought to suffice, for which your General has an app.

13 *Six V.C.s before breakfast*

At the hashtag cenotaph, performative piety stands easy while our misbegotten beachhead floats face down off Cape Helles. It's written large in the Non-Dom's daily, worn cotton-rich at the checkout. For £19.99, plus postage, this quality garment now does for a Lancashire Fusilier; some foreclosed son of a long-lost milltown. The Gallipoli Centenary T-shirt Eleven takes to the field in sizes S–XXXL, feeling good about the gesture. And why not? Shot through the neck and weighed down with kit, I can still spot a good singlet when I see one. What you have to remember is that the mills were in our blood, leaching away last before our feet could touch the ground.

14 *Vine*

Free of the 'Birdcage' in the lee of a hill, three gardeners of Salonika stand easy. Across the valley, he watches from an open tent; roots a vision that will propagate on walls for a time beyond the field gun's range. Nativities are now and the Tenth Irish Seraphim. Cookham reaches for paper and starts to work as they lay down kit to pick the first grapes they will taste fresh from the vine. Macedonia gifts a minute's joy. Then the good shepherd whistles in Golgotha for the instant that wreathes his terror in its six-second loop: Giotto, grapevine, blast and burnt-flesh, Giotto, grapevine, blast and burnt-flesh, Giotto, grapevine, blast, burnt-flesh...

15 *Clickbait*

Each evening the real work starts, not at the front but in front of it: repair the wire, recover his guts, dig that sap, patrol or raid. The detail shivers in its crump-hole, funked by a Verey's glow and the unreality of it all, its goal a cornered *Hun* to bring back alive with his terror and those photographs of home. The land itself has never been so intimately known, as you snout an earth flayed of its skin. This night gets lost to all whereabouts and a dawn that lifts too quickly at your shoulder. Reduced from subaltern to silhouette, an eye narrows on the cross-hairs, somewhere on high a lark sings and off clicks the safety-catch.

What's trending today near Loos is that football, snuck up to the line, inflated at zero hour and punted towards the slag heaps north of Lens. A tan casey bulked with rain, lace arcing to split the brow when you mistime that header. It all ends up as Great War cliché, riven and wheezing its last on the German wire. Scar tissue like this you get in one of two ways, from ball or boxing glove, today we go for a third. Some East Surrey's will steal our thunder at the Somme and this game gets all but forgotten, good luck to them. But the London Irish got there first. Men fight for the Loos Ball, going to ground at the slightest touch.

How are we to sweat our assets now the lads are sapped to bone and Belgian humus, their death-augmented realities green-screened onto memory's shonky IMAX? Ever tricky, post-production's farmed out to global partners, where Tommy's pixelated soul recurs as *Warfare 2.1*™ from the bods in Shenzhen: new features, new characters, pathos & chronotope, a shared heritage with the unseen. True to the land that bore them, the Surreys play this game as, under the field gun's brazen frenzy, the shires win their name. If love could have saved us we would not have died but die we did for all the love, post-human each, lousy with it, reeking. Please remember that you ought to remember but not like this, sweet Jesus, not like this.

Can't sing a note, not even the *Marseillaise*—oh, I'll give it a go when occasion demands—but I did have the X-Factor they were looking for. Once the press got hold of it I was an overnight sensation: the 'Heroine of Loos', a new Joan of Arc. Golden *salons*, cocked hats, bemedalled generals and the public square, as their ballyhoo broke over me. At seventeen I was that month's face-of-the-war, mounting the 'Staircase of Heroes' to the *Panthéon*, blazing my comet of a season. Sold an exclusive to *Le Petit Parisien* and got locked in some chateau to homespin thoughts for the nation. My reason for telling you? I'm not even writing this.

19 *Emoji*

When peripherals are the Heliograph, Begbie Lamp and pigeon, communication is a problem. Best stick to the runner and keep it simple, cut down on metadata, focus on the plan. Failure to spot meaning could, of course, prove lethal: the company beasted by Bergmann or Maxim, their bit-rate sputtering through flesh to close account and terminate the session. Orders, then, are for all batmen to be trained in bird duties, map reading, semaphore and message work. We want speed, fitness, care of feet, a sense of urgency and comradeship in taking turns for dangerous runs. Not a gig I'd fancy. Please destroy upon receipt and *do not* share this :-(([Sad face].

20 *Notre Dame des Brebières*

Legacies of the War to Construe All Wars: my mother *in no need of surgeons*; the hunched old woman bent into an Atlantic gale, looming out of the Connemara rain that time; my own knackered hips; me urging your pram through a hail of blossom this Spring on Miller's Lane. A national diet of wistful glory and time out of joint, no story more crooked than this, the Leaning Virgin above a town square, gilded with myth, burdened with meanings that tilt it past the horizontal. As if the random shell-damage cannot be left to lie, as if some outcome depends upon a third-rate miracle. Just press 'download' and Photoshop™ them all back to vertical.

16

21 *Commuter*

He insists we go outside to show us the moon, our two-year old pointing at his man made of cheese. By a slice of light from the half-open door I look to you; feel the gentle suck of warm air from the grate, a sudden welter of regret tugging at my lungs. God knows, our mood about the house has made such moments few and far between. *Moon, moon!* he says, as if the word holds the heft of all things. A child's finger marks the way skyward to this moment and now all roads lead to France. When I slip away at dawn, the thatch is humming with early frost, the downs roll their green path to the sea and all my Tipperaries stretch before me, unreachable, beyond.

To access more footage you can go to our website where you'll find sun, sand and skin, with the main event pixelated though viewable elsewhere. Replay the final walk, his terminal seconds, those blissful last sips from a cocktail glass. Make out the shabby clothed youth with dapper beard, unfettered by doubt as he strolls into shot by that tree to the right of the screen. It's a total artwork, so good they will hang him twice as, see, he too botches his job on the third tourist. We will crane to get into the picture, we will pose beside the garotte, claim our own tragic carnival. *Menschenmaterial* for the networks: a postcard for our times.

23 *The Show*

Audience Notes for Mametz Wood, where—during the course of this large-scale, site-specific production—you are guaranteed a vivid glimpse of our becoming through death. Check availability at the online store and if you're coming, use SatNav only as a guide. From all directions you'll end up on a single track with an uneven surface, so walk, don't run. Supported by public funding through various bodies, this is a sold-out show. Late then, I'll not make it myself but me and the lads will be there in spirit; we'll hold our absent tongues and chip in the odd chit of bone. Strictly speaking, the age guidance is 14+ though, with these things, you could always lie.

Re-fried over-easy, we're consumed as ready simile: the hardcore classic of a sopping Glastonbury, the mud-brimmed Hunters of some washed-out Latitude. Of course, your *"like the bloody Somme"* is nothing of the sort and it's not us you mean. That's Third Ypres with its limitless mud bound within the nutshell of a bullet, collapsing all context into the pulp of a pal's sniped brain. There was no bad dope or robbing Scousers, no lost mobiles or broken portaloos; though we too pissed where we could and the lines, for sure, went down. For us and one unplugged minute, there was sunshine, a cigarette and in that sunken lane, the same brief brotherhood of man.

25 *Bergsonian Numbers*

Alright then, let us assume that the sheep in a flock are identical and, for the purposes of history, all men likewise, differing only by the position they occupy on our right or left flank. Let us, indeed, set aside the fifty sheep themselves and retain but the idea of them by way of commemoration. The impression of a multiplicity of units all absolutely alike is, as you say, the product of simple intuition; caught today by a coachload of smartphones held aloft beside *Langemarck*. Number you define as a collection of units or a synthesis of one and the many, though at the end of a bayonet, as the home of a bullet, in the path of an ill-wind, every number is one.

26 *Spoiler alert*

⚠ We don't want to spoil it for everyone but crucial elements are about to be revealed, base details blurted out and the whole show ruined. It starts down the line in Heaven, where red tabs cajole us across pristine maps. Of course, they'd do it themselves or they wouldn't ask but the fact is they don't so we do, walking forward at the whistle while battle plans get knocked into bundles of bloody rags. Shell shortage, espionage, trench raid squawker or one of our pigeons caught with Haig's *billets doux*: somehow the fuckers knew. So, what screws up your afternoon's view was the Saturday we got shot. War books, games and films: ghost-written, the whole damned lot.

All we want is PAX but, man, did they unfriend or what? So here they are lined up in lip sweaters larping like their lives depend on it, flashing the swammies or shouldering a Boom Stick. And TOS was worse than TNG, totally FUBAR. It don't take no G9 to see that winter is coming to those squads: they were Bantha Fodder from the get-go, SOL. And by 1916 you got served whether you liked it or not and wound up KIA, planking in some field or MIA totally. I'm telling you, no amount of Dead Presidents would tempt me to get into that, MOH or no. It's just not my idea of a good time, just not my idea of the HOPE.

They're going out again all over Europe: the stag parties, hen nights, *No surrenders* and Day-Glo™ re-lit for our own lifetime. Dublin sucks it up with the shades of Sherwood Forest, still convinced they're in Flanders not fish in the barrel of Northumberland Road. And, as Malone and Grace ghost their way around folklore, our Poundshop™ Grey sees those dreary steeples of Fermanagh and Tyrone re-emerge to pick at the frayed strings of empire. Secretary, did they give a flying fuck when they ticked the box marked 'Go'? Your sad namesake's tattered ribbon of men splayed across the Somme. *We know what we are dying for. Thank God the day has come.*

Buy it now for two-seven-five, condition as shown in photo, too well-made to be repro, the kosher stuff of a lost patrol. As metaphors got real and euphemism ugly, the Aldershot Design lugged its rough rigging onto the dog-tired shoulders of our line. And, if you're browsing for archetype, for "how it really was", then scroll no further than this, one belt; two braces; bayonet frog; pouches for ammo; one haversack; valise with two straps and carriers for the head and helve of an E-tool. This was our hyperlink, a one-piece jacket for the universal soldier: Dai's Greatcoat, Hotspur's mail, John Ball's frayed thread for the fucked-up Grail of Mametz Wood. Epic failure/epic fail.

Christmas Past is Christmas Present, strolls Mesopotamia mobile in hand, buffering the orange bundle of a man beyond meaning. So at Kut we stick it out with the Poonas, waiting on the RFC's hand-dropped payload; tight in the hair's breadth between whizz-bang and telegram. The text-speak of a Field Service Postcard says enough: *we dnt cm in2 yr cts as conkrez or nmes but libr8rs*. Though, if needs be, we'll be back in black with a South London twang, in biplane or bomb-vest, to stroll into markets or drop in on uncivilized tribes. Repeat then, repeat: *Kill them all. God will know His own.* Each man blessed with just enough afterlife to teach him they were wrong.

17

31 *MOOC*

According to them as knows, every letter is negotiable. What, then, is *massive* about 'brisk' fighting or 'stern' opposition: 100, 1,000, 10,000? You can smell the frontline long before you see it and *open* is out where you don't want to be, lest you supply that stench for the living. *Online*, for sure, is where we're at, three of 'em: front; support; and reserve, a wet populous dyke stretching from Flanders to the Somme. *Course* is orders and, orders is orders, as in 'there is no other course open to us but to fight it out', so we attack at first light, where the line is weakest and wastage low. Any questions? Yes you. 'Begging your pardon, Sir, what have we learned from this?'

32 *School Run*

If you've a minute, tweet this: the car-struck badger you've driven past these last two weeks, *pikelhaube* snout irate in death, body bloating with fetid air, hind-legs rigid in surrender. *Kamerad*, emptied of essence, this is the boy from your home village, that snotty kid with a terrier whose Dad liked a drink; the one who pissed himself when Miss Manning caught him with a rat in his desk. Him. Always the last to put up his hand, always unlucky in love. His losing streak continued over here and now that's him rotting away to your left, hung on the brambles of a B-road: a passing stain in no man's land, fuel for the coming spring. He'll walk no more on Cotswold.

33 *Neurasthenia*

No generation for your overshare, we hashtag it inward, keep the secret to ourselves until the back door slams or the coalman drops a sack. Only once, when some drayman lost his grip, did the street get it out of me. One time and one time only, as I shuffled to *The King's Arms* and that big word which claimed our captain revived my cowardice. Before I punched him, Stan's kid laughed at "the man with the muck rake" while I pissed time down my leg. Never again. Though back in the mud of a moment, my allotment stays undug as I listen to the larks. And each night beside the po, I am cured by persuasion from a ghost-racked wife.

On CCT, I see him stab and stab again a well-killed kid from the next estate: little warrior, cock of the walk. Subaltern of the seventeen streets and their respawn army; his boys held this patch, his boys hold it still: from the Met, from the blacks from the *who-you-fucking-looking-at?* The trench is well-established as, there beyond the bypass, attrition starts where the sun goes down and the gates begin. His family has been informed and somewhere a comedian is perfecting the voice: *you is, like, dead meat innit, Blood?* Remember, if you missed the show you can catch up online, though we must warn you the following contains scenes you may find disturbing.

For want of explanation, you order a pun to stand-to and serve that teatime with some reason. Was his *Call of Duty*® too strong; did it box him in? Night after night the same game teases the hunger of his brain, shits him out on the far side of meaning, lethal scenarios unspooling into Tetris sleep. Black Ops, Ghosts, tea or coffee, kill or be killed? A thousand options fuse into crazy nitre, his mother's call across their No Man's Land of the staircase, where once per second a pixel misses its aim. This little soldier's virtual officer logs another 'Self-Inflicted Wound' though a glance around the bedroom door is enough to register that he's lying when he writes home: 'Tim died smiling.'

With six new eps, the national ghost goes primetime. Watch as he walks through history's sand-bagged wall, script bayonet-sharp and bug eyes fixed upon the evening's objective: go forth and bring a hint of comic perspective to this misbegotten show. It's a cunning plan, high risk that's true, but if it's going to work then the cheap-seat music hall of the 1980s and the decade's favourite clown is the thing to pull it off. Don't be shocked. This stuff works and we laugh a lot, dabbing tears through the season finale, as Baldrick and Blackie and Darling and George charge slow-mo to fade, their underpants and pencils and madness ignored.

Log on to see that our next gig is Vimy Ridge but, before we head off, let's get a few things straight: DON'T say 'team member', DO say 'independent supplier of offensive services'; DON'T say 'recruitment', DO say 'onboarding'; DON'T say 'uniform', DO say 'kit'. Instead of 'losses', consider casualties our 'fee per delivery'. 'Appliance' will more than suffice when referring to the mix of phosgene and chlorine. On no account confuse 'brisk' with 'bloodbath' when reporting back to High Command, likewise 'termination' with 'death'. In both cases men shall be deemed 'unavailable'. Don't forget that this is what you signed up for, this what buys those homes fit for heroes.

So let us consider the maths. By the age of 92, the Second World War widow honoring a father's Gallipoli, has shifted around 30,000 poppies for the Legion over a period of 76 years. Now divide that by ten and arrive at the approximate number of mailings in a twelve-month period. Multiply that by the number of years since a nation outsourced its kindness then throw in the daily cold calls. Of the charities sampled 99 possessed her details, 70 of which had got them from third parties, 21 'assumed' permission to share based upon her not opting out. Everyone maximizing data. Everyone just getting on. And she did leave a number: *Please phone 999 elderly lady gone over cliff.*

Alas, the young master shan't live to accede, borne off on a hand-cranked reel of grainy pals, Lee-Enfields at port. His sister, likewise, loses her chap, leaves home for a VAD and never comes back, all changed, changed utterly itself to past. A welter of duties, those uppity proles and it's gone for good. The tea gowns, breeches and a well-shot cast; that hint of scandal in the stable lad's nose; a grudging half-brother who'll be back for his dues; servants a-plenty and honey for tea; every place known and each to his own: the obseqious fetish of a national ghost. Then some right-schooled scion re-scripts the bloody lot and, in times like these, well, of course, we lap it up.

Say it's for the 'Mother Country', but we know different. Appropriated to stay awake for Allenby's push at Megiddo, we are quite the meme. Telegram to the Governor lauding how woke we are for the Turkish guns, how woke in the fight for Zion. The conundrum's built-in: both empire and burden, we are welcome and despised, sleeping but woke to the rot, our lives mattering and not. Troop-shipped to Flanders for the honour of our island, leeward to the chlorine, the phosgene, the mustard, we are mentioned in despatches. *Stay woke. Watch closely.* Truth requires no belief, fi'true, but let me tell you waking up's a damn sight harder than going to sleep.

18

41 *War Poet*

Beneath this creeping barrage squats our chap, in his breast pocket the scribbled draft that sets off a vintage look: hapless subaltern, sick with sin, chewing pencil and pity onto notepaper doomed to be found upon a mud-matted corpse. *En route* to legend, *Herr Krupp's* handiwork tears its messy path through temporal, parietal and the red wet thing of a line-break. Let us rest here a while then dig down to the destruction layer where we find change come suddenly and everywhere, and everywhere the final week of this poets' war: Boudicca's wrath, shock and awe, the stratified earth of charred words pulling free of *decorum*.

When you ask how he gets that flavour, your affable neighbour, with a flourish of the tongs says, *Iron into gold*. And the lovely new house? *Have another burger.* For his mate Dave, it's the work of an hour to encrypt a trade deal and unpin the barrels, or when running short, do the night drive to that field in Kent. Just a jaunt out of Pressburg and a trip to the shop while the kids are on *exeat* with their mothers in France. Bought legally at source, filched home to the Weald, it is but a laudable attempt to maximize returns. No nexus here just the blameless gyres of commerce. With the heat from his barbecue he starts to sweat, gets Dave's text: we're all gangsters now.

An inch either way with that selfie-stick and he'd have gotten his wish. Instead, the disfigured ghost hauled off the Salient gets a trip to Sidcup. Here, he becomes an early milestone on the road to a meme as Gillies waltzes his tube pedicle across the future of medicine, from shattered jaw to the excised strips of Walter's abdomen. Flehming into the mirrorless Twenties, this miracle of modern science still works his transfer of pheromones into a good marriage, two girls and a century later, the great-grandchild who can post: *Here is my 'duck-face' because it's the only face I know how to do. Need I be worried it might get stuck like this for life?* Child, if the wind should change…

Let's go back to the maths and their anomalous facts. Like a one-nil win with just 10% possession, it's our guilty liberal secret that, of the 2,226 poets published in the Great War for Civilisation, most of them were more up for the former and the nation than the hassle of reflecting on a Christian education. So, the *Richmond 16* are a negligible blip, one of those recurring zeroes packed off to Dyce where they're forced to break rocks or are borrowed for the name of a choral ensemble touring their poppy show around the cathedrals. Perplexingly, 88.2% of socialists got cowed into taking part, a stat that, today, gives revisionist fuel for 100% shit like this.

In the end, you'll know little more than those *poilus* baa'ing up the line at the Aisne. All you have on them is history's widescreen, and selected ironies of hindsight—Churchill's cock-up in the Dardenelles, Benito's brush with death, Gutmann's citation and the German "field rabbinate". And, while we now know the true cost of a Jewish Iron Cross or why the bells ring for Armistice as the telegram boy leans his bicycle against the gate, this is all we know. Uncle Alf wasn't telling, that's for sure, his gnosis wrapping stillness about the 6-year old jangling Pip, Squeak & Wilfred in a room that smells of baccy, piss and Black Bullets: keys to a door he'll never open.

For the price of five minutes, pick one at random from thousands at the road-side. Today, moss-kilted, a Black Watch Private on my drive to *The Hope*. Bruce, Cumming, Dass, Dearness, Esson, Gunn and then we're into Seaforths with a few Scots Guards: the men of South Ronaldsay for whom he juts a sculpted jaw. Best foot forward, knee towards the Firth, his left-hand rests where a flagstone heart would beat to not forget those unreturned to croft, estate or yole. Or the living nowheres of Hoxa, Herston, Suckquoy and Burwick, lasting a little while longer, though never such villages again. Beneath the names a scout troop wreath remains prepared.

47 *Unboxing*

Unboxed for the Channel 4 doc, DNA shadows of a lost Black Watch. You *need* to see this, right? And Lamarr will do it for you, uploading as he goes, each tease of new stuff, new features, more stuff. So, let's start in close-up with that spoon, scuffed up by the plough and our first clue: those initials, see, in sulphate blue. To regimental records then, Sophie, back to you in the lab for the delectation of fabric and bone, for that shot away femur just below the groin. This boy died slowly from loss of blood but, thanks to advances in forensic technique, we can now dial up descendants, re-gift with full honours, pan right, roll credits and fade.

Start with that photograph, then track the drift of alias through the life of one man to its resting place in time. Today, at twenty-eight, you are Nguyên the Accomplished, Thành the dishwasher, a pastry chef from Ealing at the point of becoming Quoc the Patriot, always an interloper kept out on the step. Surely, though, you stand there, borne but ignored, snapped among the old men—stern and ascetic, settling their account— still years from history's tag. Nomad, scofflaw, nondescript enigma, Zelig-at-the-shoulder of coin and salt and victor, the nascent song of rolling thunder distant down the hall: *Ho, Ho, Ho Chi Minh/ Ho, Ho, Ho Chi Minh.*

The conditions, in accordance with which the plebiscite herein before provided for, are laid down in the Annex hereto. It should be noted that any decision to withdraw is taken according to the constitutional requirements of the state concerned and thus takes into account all possible consequences, including for the individual citizen. Secession shall take back all mines within the Basin; all bananas straight or bent; all cheese, wine and border crossing; potatoes; bread; the Pound Sterling or Saar franc; the right to say 'No' and mend our nets; frontiers; compassion. The *reich* may be rejoined only when a clear majority has been returned from among its people.

Sometimes your own ghost joins them, dressing left from the undone years of your twenties. A tennis ball pings off the back wall of the old *Kongressehalle,* as fathers coach precocious children in the latest craze. Out front, you stand at that lectern, your brain's frantic CGI pixelating the century's other great set-piece; ordering the ranks, channelling the ghosts toward a powerless insight. Later, beside the ovens, you quarrel with a New York Jew before both of you collapse exhausted into a borrowed tent. What takes you, then, to the woods at 2AM to go fuck the nameless moonlight of each other through to dawn?

"I just think a century's gone by and
we're somewhere else in the story."
                    – Glyn Maxwell, *On Poetry*.

NOTES

Generally, I'm inclined to agree with Basil Bunting that notes are an admission of failure. Like him, however, I acknowledge that they may also allay small irritations for those readers curious enough to want to follow through on some of the allusions and reference-points for these poems. I offer them, then, merely to point search engines in the right direction. The pieces are written to survive alone so if you feel that you need these notes, you are likely to feel also that I have failed on some level. If you're simply curious, what follows are general reference points, supplied where I think most helpful, with numbers corresponding to the poems, in the case of those from *The Unreturning* sequence. I hope they add interest to a reading in whatever way such details may do. With David Jones's *In Parenthesis* and Eliot's *The Waste Land*, there is, at least, some precedent for supplying fulsome notes to a Great War subject. Consoling myself with this fact, I duly clamber onto the shoulders of giants.

'Let Us Sleep Now': at the end of U-Bahn Line 3, Simmering is the location of one of the city's main cemeteries.

'Phoebus Apollo': 'Phoebus Apollo' were Grenfell's last words as a shaft of sunlight shone through a gap in the curtains of his room.

'Trench Requisites': During the Great War the main London department stores had a 'Trench Requisites' section where soldiers, bound for the front, went to stock up on an array of useful items and small luxuries.

'Knight Errant, 1915': 'Knight Errant (Self-Portrait)' was finished in Vienna around March 1915, just prior to Kokoschka's departure for military service and six months before he was badly wounded in Galicia.

'An-Sky's Lament': An-Sky was a Russian-Jewish author, playwright, researcher of Jewish folklore, polemicist, and cultural and political activist. He urged Jewish intellectuals to collect whatever information they could on the Jewish wartime experience for fear that, if left to others, it would be obliterated. The quote is verse 14 from Psalm 44.

'Turnip Winter': The harsh winter of 1916–1917, known in Germany as "the Turnip Winter" ('Steckrübenwinter'), was one of extreme food shortages, social unrest and civilian suffering.

'The 1st Women's Battalion of Death': This was the first women's combat battalion to be organised in Russia just after the abdication of the Tsar in 1917, following a petition by the three times decorated Maria Bochkareva to the Minister of War Alexander Karensky. Despite their bravery in battle—often outstripping the efforts of their male comrades—the women's battalions faced indifference from the authorities and open hostility from many of the men. Bochkareva herself was executed by the Bolsheviks in 1920.

'Wanton Boys': This poem is hugely indebted to Cecil Lewis's memoir of his time in the RFC, *Sagittarius Rising*. 'PBI' stood for 'Poor Bloody Infantry'. 'Nacelle', 'Pitôt tube', 'ailerons' and 'magneto' were all technical features of the planes he flew in.

'Mallory': Having served with the Royal Artillery, the legendary climber, George Leigh-Mallory, survived the war only to go missing along with Sandy Irvine just short of the summit of Everest on the ill-fated expedition of 1924. The question of whether they made it to the top remains a mystery though theories abound. Having been lost for 75 years, his body was discovered by Conrad Anker in May 1999. He was Robert Graves's schoolmaster at Charterhouse and best man at his wedding to Nancy Nicholson.

'War And The Farmer': I am grateful to the National Trust for Scotland for the commission of this poem and the loan of James Keith's fascinating memoir *Fifty Years of Farming* (London: Faber and Faber, 1954), from which much of this text is gleaned. 'Grieve' is the north-east of Scotland term for a farm manager.

'Ripon Work': On March 21st, 1918, in the same week that Wilfred Owen turned twenty-five and rented his attic room in a cottage on Borage Lane, the Germans began their huge Spring offensive. Whilst in Ripon, between 12th March and June 5th, he worked on many of his best-known poems and roughed out his Preface.

'Nostos': In Greek epic poetry, the *nostos* was a warrior's homecoming after war.

The Unreturning

1. The title phrase comes from Paul Fussell's description of a predominant creative mind-set in *The Great War and Modern Memory*.

3. A black, six-cylinder, Gräf & Stift Double-Phaeton was the car carrying Franz Ferdinand when he was shot in Sarajevo on June 28th, 1914. The poem also alludes to a news story about Jeremy Clarkson from the *Daily Mirror* in May 2014.

4. H.M.S. *Amphion* was the first ship of the Royal Navy to be lost in the First World War, on 6th August 1914. Among its casualties were crew from the German mine-layer, *SMS Königin Luise*, which it had just sunk but which had laid the mine it struck that, in turn, sunk it. *Katabasis* is here used in its literary context of a descent into the Underworld.

6. Kitchener died in 1916, when his ship *H.M.S. Hampshire* hit a mine off Marwick Head on Orkney while he was on a diplomatic mission to Russia.

7. The title is a line from the Nick Drake song, 'From The Morning'. It is also the epitaph on his gravestone at Tanworth-in-Arden, Warwickshire. He attended Marlborough College.

9. YOLO is an acronym for "you only live once". The phrase and acronym are both used in youth culture and music, and were popularized by the 2011 song *The Motto* by rapper Drake. 'ROFL' is, likewise, a shortening of the phrase 'Rolling On The Floor Laughing'.

10. The poem alludes to a Sainsbury's advert broadcast over Christmas 2014. Its coda references a brief selection of the many proxy wars fought by the UK, with varying degrees of official recognition, in the ensuing century. '*Adoo*' is from the Arabic for 'enemy' or 'foe', most specifically, in this case, it is the name for the guerilla movement in Oman *circa* 1970.

11. All of these rumours were circulated during the Great War, except the last three which were famous non-stories from the 1980s, put out by *The Sunday Sport*, *The Weekly News* and *The Sun*, respectively: "World War 2 Bomber Found On Moon", "Adolf Hitler Was A Woman" and "Freddie Starr Ate My Hamster". *The Sunday Sport* later followed up with the headline, "World War 2 Bomber Found On Moon Vanishes".

12. The 'majority illusion' is a recently identified phenomenon of social networks, whereby an individual's decisions—from what product to buy to whether to engage in risky behaviour—often depend on the choices, behaviours, or states of other people. The illusory consensus of social media can, therefore, create dangerous perceptions of peer conformity.

13. This is virtually a found poem from a so-called 'quality' newspaper advert for product commemorating the centenary of the Gallipoli landings in 2015.

14. 'The Birdcage' was the name given to the extensive barbed-wire entanglements used on the Macedonian Front in the Great War. 'The Gardeners of Salonika' was the mocking nickname ascribed to the allied forces entrenched around Thessaloniki.

16. The Loos Football can still be seen in the regimental museum of the London Irish Rifles. It's been pawed over a lot during the years of the centenary commemoration.

17. 'True to the land that bore them / The Surreys played the game' is a quote from the poem by 'Touchstone' of *The Daily Mail* in honour of Wilfred Nevill, Commander of 'B' Company of the East Surreys who was responsible for the famous 'Football Charge' on the first day of the Somme.

18. Émilienne Moreau was a high-profile French heroine from the Great War. She enjoyed the era's equivalent of celebrity status.

19. The Heliograph and Begbie Lamp were—along with carrier pigeons—common methods of battlefield communication.

Bergmann and Maxim were makes of German machine-gun. The order for all batmen to receive training to be runners was a real one.

20. Refers to The Golden Virgin on the Basilica at Albert. It became a visual icon of the Great War, as well as providing a target practice opportunity for the artillery of both sides.

22. In 1916, the Italian nationalist, Cesare Battisti, was hung and garotted by the Austrians in his hometown of Trento. An image of his hanging corpse was then distributed on a postcard by way of propaganda. See also, Karl Kraus's 1919 play 'The last days of mankind'. *Menschenmaterial,* means, literally, 'human material'.

23. Like 'Six V.C.'s Before Breakfast', this is virtually a found poem from advertising copy for a site-specific commemorative event. The 'chit of bone' references the Owen Sheers poem 'Mametz Wood'.

24. 'Context collapse' is a concept used by academics writing about the effects of social media. It refers to the infinite audience possible online as opposed to the limited groups a person normally interacts with face to face. Social media technologies collapse multiple audiences into single contexts, making it difficult for people to use the same techniques online that they do to handle the multiplicity of face-to-face conversation.

26. The phrase 'knocked into bundles of bloody rags' comes from a speech Churchill made in 1916 to the House of Commons in connection with the high casualty rate on the Western Front.

27. I'm afraid you're on your own here. If you don't know the acronyms and want to find out, I recommend a jargon-buster app. They're real, apparently. Enjoy.

28. The title refers to the erstwhile Secretary of State for Northern Ireland, James Brokenshire. The 'dreary steeples of Fermanagh and Tyrone' is taken from famous a speech by Churchill made in 1922 about the Irish situation as it was in 1914.

'Grey' is Sir Edward Grey, British Foreign Secretary on the eve of the Great War. The closing quote is Michael Malone's alleged words when sending home two young rebels for their safety during the Easter Rising. The Sherwood Foresters were the company coming under fire in Northumberland Road. Many of the young volunteers died thinking they'd been landed in France.

30. The text message is an adaptation of part of General Maude's Proclamation of Baghdad, made on the 17th March 1917 during the Mesopotamian Campaign. The lines were famously re-invoked on the eve of the Second Gulf War in 2003. *Kill them all, God will know his own* is a phrase attributed to the Abbot of Citeaux, Arnaud Amalric, who commanded the Pope's army at the sack of Béziers in 1209, during the Albigensian Crusade.

31. A massive open online course (MOOC) is an online course aimed at unlimited participation and open access via the web. The wet populous dyke description is a quote from R.H. Tawney's 'Some Reflections of a Soldier', published in *Nation*, October 1916. The quotation comes from Haig's Special Order of the Day, issued on April 11th, 1918. As Paul Fussell points out, *brisk* had quite a precise meaning in official communiques: that about fifty per of a company had been killed or wounded in a raid.

32. There are a few ghost lines here but the main one, which closes the poem, references Ivor Gurney's 'To His Love'.

34. Aristeia is a scene in the dramatic conventions of epic poetry where a hero in battle has his finest moments (*aristos* = "best"). The opening line references Herbert Read's poem 'The Happy Warrior'

35. 'Permadead' is an expression from computer gaming in which player characters that die are *permanently* dead, removed from the game and may no longer be used to play. The poem references Wilfred Owen's 'S.I.W.' and a tragically true news item from 2015.

38. The poem refers to another tragic news story from 2015, involving Britain's oldest poppy seller, the details of which can be looked up. Barring one detail, the suicide note is verbatim.

40. 'Woke' is a political term of African American origin, referring to a perceived awareness of issues concerning social and racial justice. The British West Indies Regiment was a unit of the British Army during the First World War, formed from volunteers from British colonies in the West Indies. They distinguished themselves at the Battle of Megiddo and elsewhere in Palestine, as well as on the Western Front. The poem adapts quotes from Erykah Badu, the black American soul singer credited with reviving its current usage, and J. Saunders Redding's record of a comment made by an African American United Mine Workers official in 1940. I am aware of the cross hairs between allyship and my own cultural appropriation, here. That is the point.

41. The Krupp family were a prominent German dynasty from Essen, they became famous for their production of steel, artillery, ammunition, and other armaments in both world wars. The 'destruction layer' is a stratum found in the excavation of an archaeological site showing evidence of destruction, either by natural causes (for example earthquakes), or as a result of a military action.

42. The title alludes to Emmerich Kálmán's pro-war operetta 'Gold gab ich für Eisen' (I Gave Gold for Iron). The material comes from a gun-running news item of April 2016. The Slovakian town alluded to is Partizânske. Pressburg was the Austro-Hungarian name for Bratislava.

43. Sir Harold Delf Gillies (1882–1960) was an otolaryologist widely considered the father of plastic surgery. During World War One he worked out of the new Queen's Hospital at Sidcup. 'Duck face' is a trend of photographic pose well known on social networks. The 'flehmen response' is an animal behaviour of the mouth often held for several seconds, the main function of which is intraspecific sexual communication by transferring air containing pheromones to a chemosensory organ between the palate and the roof of the mouth.

44. 88.2% was the percentage ironically offered by comedian Vic Reeves when he said: "88.2% of statistics are made up on the spot."

45. 'Combat Gnosticism' is the concept propounded by James Campbell in his 1999 article, *Combat Gnosticism: The Ideology of First World War Poetry Criticism*, as a means of describing what he sees as the limiting notion that 'combat represents a qualitatively separate order of experience that is difficult if not impossible to communicate to anyone who has not undergone an identical experience'. Hugo Gutmann was the Jewish List adjutant who recommended Adolf Hitler for his First-Class Iron Cross. Pip, Squeak and Wilfred were the nicknames given to the three campaign medals awarded to men who had seen service in WW1.

46. 'Synecdoche' is a figure of speech in which a part is used for the whole or the whole for a part, the special for the general or the general for the special.

47. Unboxing is the unpacking of new products, especially high-tech consumer products, where the process is captured on video and uploaded to the web.

48. Responds to a photograph of future North Vietnamese leader Ho Chi Minh who attended proceedings at Versailles, aged 28, in a delegation attempting to gain some recognition for the struggle of the then Indochina against French Imperialism.

49. The poem interpolates text from Articles 50 of The Treaty of European Union and The Treaty of Versailles which set up the allied annexation of the Territory of the Saar Basin in 1920. Following a plebiscite in 1935, the citizens of the territory voted overwhelmingly to re-join the German Reich under Hitler.

50. A true story.